Magical Self-Care

The Sisters Enchanted®

Magical Self-Care

A 21 Day Expedition to Soul Field Guide

Cast boundaries, create a strong foundation and conjure a life that supports you in every way

Sara Walka

ISBN 979-8-9858148-2-8 (Hardback)
ISBN 979-8-9858148-0-4 (Paperback)
ISBN 979-8-9858148-1-1 (Digital)

Cover Design By Danielle Capri
Book Layout and Photography by Danielle Capri
Typeset in Marion and Futura PT

March 2022

A very special thank you to all of the students and community at The Sisters Enchanted® and to everyone who has helped me breathe life into this dream:

Anna Tower, Marcie Gara, Kevin Walka, Chad Tower, Christina Boos, Megan Theiner, Sarah Milne, Danielle Capri, Brandy Shaffer, Nick MacDonald, Kiara Boggs, Jen Sankey, Nikki Jastrom, Danielle Faulkner, Alicia Wands, Amber Liskey, Kelly Sroka, Pati Diaz, Emily Morrison, Valinda Cochella, Richelle Ross, Traci Bray, Carol Lee, and Amanda Meza.

Here's to many more years of magic to come!

TABLE OF CONTENTS

Welcome   13

What Is An Expedition To Soul Field Guide   16
    Why 21 days?   19
    Self-care is an act of Witchery, Remembering,
       and Rebellion   21
    Reflection   25

How To Use This Book   27

Part One: Introduction   29
    Day 1: Barriers   32
    Day 2: Boundaries   34
    Day 3: The Chaos   36
    Day 4: The Future   38
    Day 5: Time   40
    How to Take Control of Your Time   42
    Day 6: More Time   43
    How to do a Time Audit   46
    Day 7: The Quest Pack   48
    Suggested Self-Care Activities   52

Cultivate A Quest Pack   55

Part Two: Creating The Practice   63

   Day 8: Self-Care Audit   65

   Identifying Avoidance Masked as Self-Care   67

   Day 9: Practical   68

   Day 10: Spiritual   70

   Day 11: Physical   72

   Day 12: Relational   74

   Day 13: When?   77

   Day 14: Planning   81

   Tips As You Prepare To Put Self-Care Into Action   82

   More Self-Care Suggestions To Try   84

Part Three: Living the Practice   87

   Day 15: Reflection   90

   Day 16: Reflection   92

   Day 17: Reflection   94

   Day 18: Reflection   96

   Day 19: Reflection   98

   Day 20: Reflection   100

   Day 21: Reflection   102

   Additional Self-Care Suggestions   106

About The Sisters Enchanted   111

Available Programs   113

About Sara Walka   115

"My darling girl, when are you going to realize that being normal is not necessarily a virtue? It rather denotes a lack of courage!"

- Aunt Frances, Practical Magic

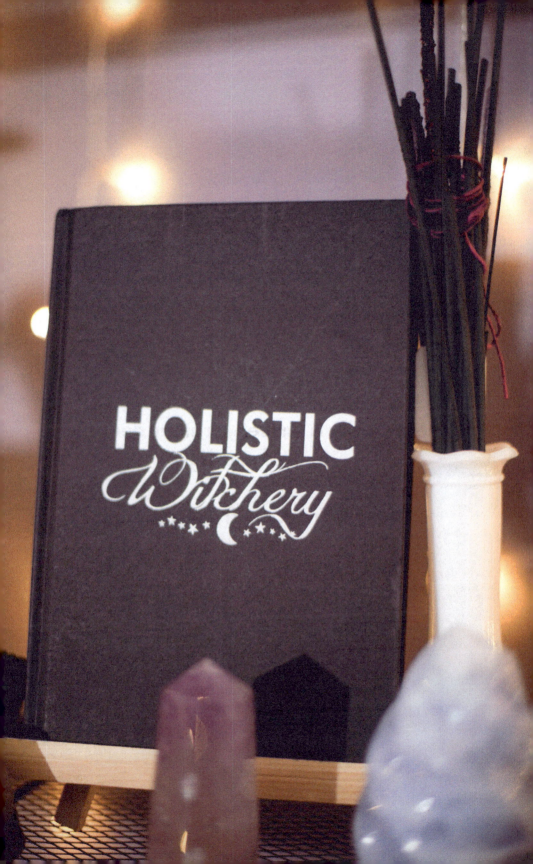

WELCOME

WELCOME

For seven years, I took my kids to visit a huge pig at a farm market.

We usually saw this pig once, sometimes twice per year. We affectionately dubbed it the *"big stinky piggy."*

The second to last time we saw this pig, it was sleeping up against a fence, and the fence had begun cracking along the bottom. We thought for sure the pig was nearing the end of its days.

A few months later, we went to see that pig again. But this time in its pen, we saw a *"Hippo the Pig"* sign on top, but instead, there were goats.

We looked all around and couldn't find the pig anywhere. Assuming the pig had passed on to its next soul adventure, we made our farm market purchases. My grandmother stopped someone who worked at the farm and asked about the pig on the way out.

It turned out that the pig had been relocated to a greenhouse in another area within the farm.

Naturally, we went to see the *"big stinky piggy."*

For seven years, we'd visited this pig, and it had always been lying in the mud, sometimes sleeping, sometimes snacking from its seemingly favorite position on the ground.

This time, the pig was standing. Not only was the pig standing, but it was walking about and grazing on all sorts of food.
I couldn't believe it!

My kids were beside themselves with happiness. My 83-year-old grandmother was thrilled, and I did what any mom of young kids in 2021 would do. I whipped out my phone and started taking lots of photos.

It's amazing what a change of scenery did for that big stinky pig.

If you find yourself stuck in the same metaphorical mud each day, do something to shake things up.

You probably don't have to go live in a greenhouse like Hippo the Pig. Maybe a walk in a new park, a fresh candle, or moving the furniture and removing stagnant energy will do the trick.

The amount of possibility, wonder, and enchantment that can come from the simplest of change is amazing.

We are always looking for the next magical thing to do, the next tarot spread or ritual idea.

But sometimes, the biggest magic is made in shaking up the mundane.

Hi, I'm Sara. I believe that intention, intuition, and everyday magic will change the world.

I founded The Sisters Enchanted® in 2016 to do just that. *Change the world.*

As of the writing of this book, we've helped tens of thousands of people see through the fog of indecision, wrong turns taken, and bring intention, intuition, and everyday magic to their lives.

Welcome to your 21-day Self-Care Practice, Magic Maker.

WHAT IS AN EXPEDITION TO SOUL FIELD GUIDE

Expedition to Soul® is a program that has reached over 60,000 people as of the writing of this book. Created by myself and hosted by my company, The Sisters Enchanted®, we do something unlike anything else available in the world of online education.

We invite participants to investigate what it is that their inner voice and compass are whispering right now. We provide the tools to assist folks in seeing the next step forward on their journey through life.

The program is *open-ended* and has different results for each participant.

This book is a **Field Guide to self-care** and follows the principles of our Expedition to Soul program.

The results are unique to each participant
The language and invitations will mean different things
to different people
There is not a 'right way' to implement, access, or receive
the information - there is only your way

To register for the next Expedition to Soul program, go to the free resources page, or scan this QR code:

"I think one of the biggest misconceptions of self-care is that it has to be a big 'thing'~ I often use shopping as a tool (crutch) but that's not really taking care of myself ~ it's often adding to my problems. True self-care are the moments that you can take each day ~ 15 mins to go outside and ground yourself, a cup of coffee or tea with zero distractions (NO phone/ social media), a bath or shower with your favorite soaps, lotions, etc."

-Nikkii

The Sisters Enchanted
Community Member

On a scale of 1-10 (1 being not great and 10 being excellent), how would you rate self-care in your life right now?

The answer will probably vary based on the day, what's going on for you energetically*, and how supported you feel at any time.

Self-care is a term and idea that has become all the rage over the past few years and leaves many feeling like they will never have the self-care moments that are plastered across beautiful Instagram feeds.

In fact, self-care has become a $450 billion market according to one source, iriworldwide.com.

Here's what self-care is not:
- Something that needs to look a certain way to be impactful
- One size fits all
- A time-consuming practice that requires specific acts or items

Here's what self-care is:
- An invitation to check in with yourself, identify what is really going on for you, and release the heavyweight of expectation
- Anything that leaves you feeling cared for, rested, or clear

Here's a radical proposal: ***What if your entire life is a container for self-care?***

You hit bumps in the road, take left turns when you meant to go right, and still, at the end of the line, your life is a container for self-care.

As you meander through this Field Guide on self-care, I invite you to consider that radical proposal.

*What do I mean when I use words like energy or energetically? This is how you feel on a deep level. Your physical, spiritual, and emotional bodies are all put together to form your energy. You have your own energy blueprint and energetic connections to the people and things around you.

WHY 21 DAYS?

It is said to take 21 days to form a new habit (by some, others disagree entirely).

21 days is about *three weeks of a lunar cycle or of a menstrual cycle* so it matches the energy of change and movement with *one week for rest and reflection.*

21 numerologically adds up to become the number three, and three is a powerful number in magic and the human consciousness. Great literature, fairy tales, folktales, and mythology often give the characters three tries or three lessons. It is a number with deep roots in how we think, talk, and learn without even knowing it.

For 21 days, we will embark on this self-care journey in **three different parts**.

SELF-CARE AS AN ACT OF WITCHERY, REMEMBERING, AND REBELLION

By the end of this experience, you will understand how to create a life that is a container for self-care. You will also have plenty of ideas for taking a few precious moments to care for yourself in the thick of life.

SELF-CARE AS AN ACT OF WITCHERY, REMEMBERING, AND REBELLION

Learning to live in rhythm with a self-care practice is the ultimate act of witchery, remembering, and rebellion. We are taught to do as we're told, work hard, and follow the leader from a young age.

Making space to hear your inner truth, be your own guiding light, and live intentionally is the exact opposite of the cadence we are accustomed to marching to.

In remembering what true joy feels like, you will find what you are looking for. It can be found while reclaiming passion and delight, sprinkling moments throughout your day that leave you feeling powerful and magical and feeling like the fabulous person you were born to be.

I love the word witchery because it causes a stir within the soul. Some people hear the word and cringe because of mainstream assumptions about it and the folks who claim it. Some hear the word and get curious. Others hear it and immediately feel alive.

Wherever you fall on that spectrum, know that there is something for you in whichever way you are feeling. There is something to be uncovered, something to run toward and investigate, and something to be gained.

Stepping into union with your own well-being is powerful. You will remember when you last felt alive, happy, and whole. You will remember all the times somebody took advantage of you. You will remember yourself. You will rebel against the status quo and the belief that you must run yourself ragged to be worthy and upstanding.

At the end of this **21-day Practice**, you will be ready for whatever the next step on your journey through life is.

And it will be *amazing*.

"Self-care is my jam! I like to follow the natural rhythm of the new and full moon. When I schedule my self-care days (which are non-negotiable) around the new and full moon, I guarantee myself that every 2 weeks, I am doing something special for ME. I self-assess and see what my souls needs, what my body needs, and what my mind needs and go from there. It is also so important to have grace with yourself. There will be times you miss a 'date with yourself,' and that's ok. Remember, the way you love yourself is how you treat others to love you."

-Maritza

The Sisters Enchanted
Community Member

Whether you're a busy mom of young kids, a person with a spacious life and plenty of opportunities, or a retired person facing down the tunnel of the unknown, everything in this book applies to you. Consider this an invitation to find areas in your life that you haven't seen before.

All examples provided in this book are a *spectrum of experience*.

For example, having too much time can be just as great a barrier as not having enough time.

Having a very chaotic life can cause some folks to shut down while others thrive under the same circumstances.

Spending time alone in the bathtub sounds like bliss for some and a complete waste of time for others.

Too often, we look at ideas specifically as presented and don't allow ourselves the creative flexibility to discover what we can learn from them. If an example involves someone who works 40 hours per week and you don't, this doesn't mean you can't take something from that example and apply it to yourself.

Be flexible, creative, and dig for your own gems in this book. I promise you'll find them if you're open to it.

Quick note: You'll find words like magic, witchery, and enchantment in this book. While some folks may hesitate a little upon reading them, I want you to know that these concepts, ideas, and practices are whatever you believe them to be and nothing more. I know that this world is full of beautiful people seeking a life that feels delightful, spacious, and on purpose. You are welcome here, **Magic Maker**.

REFLECTION

What do you stand to lose if you don't care for yourself?

As humans, we tend to look for the thing we stand to gain, but what's more important (and more helpful in moving forward) is what we stand to lose.

The emotional connection to the things we don't yet have or have yet to experience is weaker than the one we have to what we already know.

Most of us attach like a steel rope to what we already have and what we've already experienced.

So, what do you stand to lose if you don't care for yourself? Here's a *peek at my list*:

- The ability to hike and see the world from the top of a mountain
- Time having fun with my family and laughing until I cry
- Creative thinking that comes from an unburdened mind
- A flexible work/life schedule that allows for time and location freedom
- The hope that I will, one day, achieve some huge and very audacious goals

List yours out before moving forward.

"My favorite form of self-care is my 'zen time.' My partner thankfully understands that when I make the statement that I need a minute to zen, he respectfully lowers the volume of everything in the house and lets me alone until I come back. It really helps reset my energy! My one bathroom with a tub has been out of commission, but I would take baths to help reset and relax as well.

And a tip for self-care is honestly to start setting boundaries. Once you establish what you will and will not allow around you helps make you feel so much better after the lines are drawn."

-Amber

The Sisters Enchanted
Community Member

HOW TO USE THIS BOOK

This book will help you create a self-care practice and provide you with plenty of space for reflection and connection to your current and desired life.

You can use this book in a few ways:
- Read through the entire book first and then go back to the beginning and complete the prompts one by one.
- Open the book to **Day 1** and begin there without knowing what's to come! Set a reminder for yourself on your phone, calendar, or email to complete one reflection each **day for 21 days.**
- Schedule in one month for each of the three sections of the book and complete the reflections and suggestions slowly over a three months rather than a three weeks
- Or, whatever way works best for you! It's your book after all.

You may even want to purchase a separate journal and go through the activities twice per year or each year beginning on your birthday or some other meaningful event for you.

The topics and reflections in this book are ones that you will undoubtedly need to dust off from time to time.

Whatever you choose to do and however you choose to use this book, be sure to make it work for you. The book is not meant to be something that leads you to feel guilty. You'll get what you need from it at just the right time.

Part One:

INTRODUCTION

Days 1–7
Laying the Foundation for Self Care

Magical Self-Care

PART ONE: INTRODUCTION

Throughout days 1 through 7, you will lay the foundation for your 21-day Self-Care Practice. This section will lead you through self-reflection and what is known as *Shadow Work*.

Shadow Work is the act of examining the parts of self that you might not be aware of or actively try to avoid. This can include past experiences or stories that you hold onto, such as self-sabotaging thoughts or behaviors.

Hard truth time - you may even find yourself face-to-face with excuses in this section. We all do it.

What's important is that you remain open to possibilities.

This section will help you see why your life may or may not feel like it is currently supporting you. When I say that I want your life to feel like a container for self-care, you shouldn't have to go looking for self-care. It should be built into your life. I want you to feel empowered to make decisions that leave you feeling fulfilled and joyful.

At the end of this section, you will understand what is standing between you and a life that feels like a container for self-care.

DAY 1: BARRIERS

Common barriers to a self-care practice include time, caregiving, and energy levels. They stand between where we are and where we want to be. The thing about these barriers, though, is that they are ones that we build in our minds.

By this, I mean that we get to decide just how great the barrier is. Are we making it out to be a six-foot brick wall with barbed wire running along the top, or is it a small stream that you can hop right over to get to the other side?

Depending on your perception and lived experience, each barrier you have standing between you and your self-care practice will feel a certain way. It might feel impossible to get past or feel like a minor inconvenience.

Even the biggest, strongest, most impossible wall can be brought down with a plan and the right tools. The same goes for your barriers.

This **21-day Self-Care Practice** begins with barriers because these will undoubtedly be the hurdles that hold you back. You will find it challenging to enforce boundaries, that you are too tired to "*do all the things,*" or that you stop yourself in your tracks when your expectations don't meet reality.

Acknowledging these barriers from the start and planning for them can help with this. It can also help you see where you might be your own barrier (*wild, I know!*).

Here are a *few common barriers*:

- Not enough time/too much time
- Too many people to care for/nothing to care for
- Too much energy/not enough energy

Barriers are about perception. What are your past and present barriers, and how do you perceive them?

DAY 1 REFLECTION: Use this page to list the barriers you generally encounter. Common barriers include time, caregiving, lack of privacy, other people, energy, motivation, other priorities. Then, write at least one thing you can do to get past that barrier or plan for it.

If you find it challenging to come up with an idea or plan for a barrier, leave it blank. Come back later.

DAY 2: BOUNDARIES

The first thing that comes to mind for most people when the word 'boundaries' is used is the image of trying to keep something out. A boundary is protecting what's inside and everyone and everything that needs what's inside.

Think of a vegetable garden. One might create a boundary to keep animals out. The vegetables need protection to grow and feed everyone, which can be just as much a benefit to the animals being fed in the end as it is to the humans creating the boundary. Another example is the concrete blocks used to barricade roads during construction work. That is a boundary that allows work to be done. Eventually, everyone has a better driving experience on a nice road. Driving during the construction work is annoying, but in the end, the fruit of the experience is a better alternative.

Setting and maintaining boundaries is very uncomfortable because it often requires saying no, which can feel like letting others down. It might stir up some chaos if you've never set one before.

Spoiler alert: The more difficult it feels to set a boundary, the more you probably need it.

Setting boundaries in and of itself is a beautiful and necessary act of self-care.

What needs protecting? And how will it impact your life and the lives of those around you in the end? Those are the questions at hand when navigating the discomfort of setting boundaries.
Look back at your list of barriers and begin considering what

boundaries you may need to set. Don't forget to take a deep look at yourself as a barrier, too.

DAY 2 REFLECTION: In the inner circle, write out how you and the lives of those around you will benefit from the boundaries you set. On the outside of the circle, write about what the boundary might look like.

What are you saying no to? What do you need? What will you no longer be doing? How will you enforce it?

For an example, visit the free resources webpage at this link: 21dayselfcare.com

DAY 3: THE CHAOS

On days 1 and 2, you explored two crucial pieces of the self-care adventure; **barriers and boundaries**. Today you are going to put that exploration to use.

If you're here, it's probably because you need a little help in this self-care area and identify as someone whose life generally feels chaotic. Maybe you're a caregiver, and you have a job, or you're single with loads of freedom but feel like you're always running from one thing to the next.

Or maybe you feel chaos in your soul because you sit and watch time fly by while the energy within you just builds and builds with no outlet causing a deep sense of anxiousness. The chaos of life or emotion comes so fast and furious that it isn't until after the storm has passed that we realize we let it become a barrier or didn't uphold a boundary.

Our online **Holistic Witchery** program teaches a framework called **Intention to Intuition™**. It helps create a rhythm in our lives and ourselves so that chaos is less of a threat to the magical life we want to be living. For our purposes in this 21-day Magical Self-Care Practice, you will begin identifying your chaotic times.

Chaos isn't always a bad thing. It can make you feel alive and feel like you're accomplishing something in your life. It can even make you feel like you're a good person because you're so busy and able to manage so much.

In the end, though, chaos will only get you farther from where you want to be no matter what kind of chaos is lurking in your life.

DAY 3 REFLECTION: List out the different points in your day that feel utterly chaotic. Where can you cut something out, create a system or process, or get support in that area? Where do you simply need to drop expectations or let go of control?

Alternatively, suppose you find that nothing seems chaotic. What contributes to feeling overwhelmed or like you just can't seem to get moving? This is the internal or emotional chaos that is holding you back.

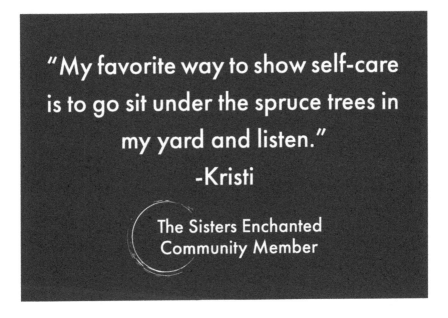

"My favorite way to show self-care is to go sit under the spruce trees in my yard and listen."
-Kristi

The Sisters Enchanted
Community Member

DAY 4: THE FUTURE

Why do you want to conjure up a magical self-care practice? Is it because someone on the internet told you you should? Or is it because you want to change something about your life?

Maybe you want to feel like you're living a life of purpose and intention, one filled with intuitive knowing and moments that are bubbling over with magic?

Whatever the reason, knowing why you are on this journey and what you hope to gain from it is going to come in handy when the going gets tough and you begin to feel down on yourself. Knowing the reason is only one ingredient in our self-care foundation potion.

The other critical component is believing.

Fiercely believing in yourself, your worth, and another way of living is possible for you are the magic ingredients and the hardest to come by.

Understand that the future really is yours and self-care can be built into it. Consider your daily life up to this point. Is it the life that will get you where you want to go? Do you even know where you want to go? Self-care is a necessary tool in finding your way and ensuring you end up in the right spot.

You've identified barriers, set boundaries, wrangled the chaos, and next, you're going to do a little future casting.

DAY 4 REFLECTION: Write about your future. Where are you? Who are you with? What are you wearing, eating, drinking, experiencing? Be as wild as you want to be with this. After all, you're the only one who has to believe it.

CHALLENGE: Do this activity while imagining yourself as the same person you are now, just as you are. You are already worthy of your future vision, Magic Maker.

"Meditation is probably my favorite because it helps slow and refocuses my thoughts. I'm an air sign and have a tendency to really overthink and let my thoughts run the show."
-Rachael

The Sisters Enchanted
Community Member

DAY 5: TIME

Barriers have been identified, boundaries set, chaos conquered, and future visions cast. Next, we move on to the topic of time. Time is your only finite resource. You can take action to heal an unhealthy body, get help with emotional burdens, and always make more money.

There is no way to recover a minute once it has passed. At The Sisters Enchanted®, the online education company I founded, it's fair to say that we are obsessed with intentionality. Being time intentional is one of our core values.

"*I don't have time*" is the reason why most people don't make a practice out of self-care. Whether you're raising kids, caring for pets, providing for aging relatives, working a taxing job, or are surrounded by unsupportive family members or friends, there's always something taking up that precious resource of time.

Sometimes, motivation and mental health stand in the way of making time for self-care. This often leads to a rabbit hole of thought, with a neon sign flashing "*shame*" at the end.

Whatever your personal thing is, know that it's valid. There is nothing wrong with you because you can't seem to make the time for self-care. Hopefully, Days 1-4 of this adventure armed you with some helpful tools as you begin unearthing the story that you are telling yourself about time and its availability (or lack thereof).

Cultivating a healthy relationship with time will eventually open the door to a healthy relationship with your self-care practice.

Doing so will lead to a healthier and happier *you*.

DAY 5 REFLECTION: Write about your relationship with time. How do you use it, waste it, try to find more of it? How do you feel when you feel like you're wasting time versus how you feel when you've been productive? Do you have any specific stories around the time that have impacted your relationship with it? Put it all down on paper.

HOW TO TAKE CONTROL OF YOUR TIME

1. Choose a calendar and schedule in all of your 'rocks.' These are the things that don't typically change and can be counted on to happen at a specific time. Rocks can also be commitments that you already know about.
2. Pick one goal or intention to focus on while moving forward with this exercise. For more help with this, visit the free resources webpage included to support your 21-day Self-Care Practice.
3. On a blank piece of paper, list out everything that you do in a day, everything on your to-do list going forward, and any tasks or activities that you'd like to be doing in a day.
4. Go through this list and identify which tasks you can delegate to others and which you can realistically delete altogether based on the one goal or intention you have identified.
5. Take what's left and start scheduling it in!

There is a deep dive into this process on the free resources webpage at 21dayselfcare.com

DAY 6: MORE TIME

Self-care doesn't have to take an entire afternoon to have a major impact. It's one of those practices with benefits that build over time. Small doses of intentional (*and, of course, magical*) self-care will create a significant result.

Continuing on the topic of time from Day Five, consider how you perceive time. So many people look at a minute as this little blip of useless space. After all, what can you accomplish in a minute?

Now consider three, five, eight minutes...when does time *no longer become useless?*

Stop to consider that for a moment.

This is how you bend time, make it work for you, and create space for the magical *and rebellious* act of self-care, no matter what. It's in rethinking what time actually means to you.

If part of your self-care practice is laying on your bed and staring at the ceiling for 20 minutes to breathe, have at it! If it looks like spending 3 minutes writing a letter of encouragement to yourself at the beginning of your day, do that!

However big or small the block of time, it's a block of time that you have to look for and create.

Once you realize that no one will hand you an hour of free time to yourself on a silver platter, it will genuinely change your life. You must sift through the 1440 minutes allotted to you each day and save some aside for your self-care practice.

DAY 6 REFLECTION: Do a time audit on yourself. This is a powerful activity to do over a two-week time period to get a complete picture, but even one day is helpful. Identify where your time is going so that you can create time for your self-care practice.

"For me, the biggest part of self-care is moving towards joy. It is easy in life to get caught up in the 'need to do' so much that everything becomes a 'have to' even when it isn't. Give yourself permission to follow the places where you are drawn, to say no things that do not serve you, allow space to just be, and to truly be in every moment. To me, self-care is mostly about awareness of what 'self' needs vs. what the outside world (and sometimes ourselves) say we need to do."
-Shannon

The Sisters Enchanted
Community Member

"Since I tend to take on people's emotions even when talking to them from afar, just taking some time to be alone and out of the stimulation of the world is my self-care. I also enjoy working on crafts, so right now, setting time aside daily to work even 5 minutes on it resets my whole self, and putting me first is self-care. And taking time away from electronics of any kind is great self-care for me and also allows me to reset. It's like these things strengthen my soul."
-Stephanie

The Sisters Enchanted
Community Member

HOW TO DO A TIME AUDIT

To be honest, completing a time audit can feel like a complete nuisance. But, the rewards are great.

The key to successfully completing a time audit is developing a strategy or choosing a plan that works for you and that you will follow through with.

Why am I suggesting this? It turns out people, in general, are terrible at judging how long it will take to do something. We tend to overestimate or underestimate and lose all sense of planning what can realistically be done in any period of time.

To better plan for self-care and make it happen, you have to know what you actually spend your time on.

And, developing a beautiful relationship with time is a meaningful act of self-care that will truly create a life that is a container for self-care.

Here are a few strategies for completing a time audit or time study:

- Print out an hourly calendar for a two-week time period. Fill it out as you go along life for two weeks.
- Use a notes app on your phone to keep a digital log of how you spend your time throughout the day. Later, transfer this to a calendar so you can visualize the chunks of time being spent.
- Record voice memos to yourself, recording what you did during a specific period. Again, transfer this to a physical calendar so you can see the time block.
- Set reminders on your phone to alert you to check in on your time study at 9 AM, 12 PM, 3 PM, 6 PM, and 9 PM.

Refer to the free resources webpage for more ideas and information on this topic at 21dayselfcare.com.

DAY 7: THE QUEST PACK

On days 1 and 2, you were tasked with considering **barriers and boundaries**. On days 3 and 4, the **chaos of the present versus the picture of the future** was given to you. On days 5 and 6, it was about **time**.

Today, you will pack a **Quest Pack**.

I mentioned earlier that I am very much obsessed with intentionality. Well, I'm also obsessed with Quest Packs.

Remember when I told you to go looking for time? Do it enough, and you'll become great at creating time out of thin air. At that point, your only barrier will be that you aren't prepared with any of the tools you love to use during your self-care practice.

The Quest Pack is the solution to that problem.

Many people talk about creating a space in the home or a sacred altar where you can be present, connect with your intuition, and cast the dreams of your future. But what if you have a small house or lots of tiny humans or pets that are constantly touching your things? What if those magical moments of time you conjured up happens when you take a short detour to a park on your way home from work?

The Quest Pack is here to save the day. Pack a box, bag, basket, or anything else with all you need for a bit of self-care. This could include your favorite journal, candle, oracle cards, crystals...anything at all (*even snacks...definitely snacks*)!

Get in the habit of keeping it nearby at all times and bask in the glory of your genius and forward-thinking when it comes time to use it.

DAY 7 REFLECTION: Make a list of everything you want to include in your quest pack, and then get it all together!

THAT'S A WRAP ON DAYS 1–7!

Setting boundaries is arguably the most vital and challenging part of a self-care practice.

Saying no to others and no to ourselves from time to time is challenging if it's not something you're used to doing.

If you're sick and tired of being sick and tired, working with time can feel like a big mountain to climb.

Here's the thing — small steps count, and minor changes lead to big ones over time. Meet yourself exactly where you are right now.

I refer to this as a practice throughout this book because that's precisely what it is, a **21-day Magical Self-Care Practice**.

We are practicing as we create a life embedded with self-care, and we practice it as often as possible.

I will never forget the time I sat on my kitchen floor in a puddle of tears with a toddler climbing up my back and a baby in my lap. I couldn't imagine living a life that felt like there was room to care for myself at that moment.

Looking back, I can trace the steps I took to make my progress. The hard conversations, the schedule changes, and the expectations released are all little things that led to a life that feels a whole lot more spacious than it did when I was staring at a dirty floor with a river of tears dropping from my face.

You'll come back to **Part One** again and again, just like I do. For now, it's time to move on to the next section.

"Self-care is my gig. I think the biggest factor is to be unapologetic about it when you need it. I am not afraid to change my mind, say no when I need to or walk away from something that makes me feel less than magical.

I take a bath with herbs, oils, and candles. I set time aside to pull a card or two. When I'm doing a hard assignment for school, I light a wonderful-smelling candle. On cold, gloomy days, I deep clean my house, light some candles, say some things I'm grateful for and sage my space. If my family gets to be too much, my Aquarius moon helps me walk away guilt-free from things getting to be too much.

I say many, many, many affirmations throughout the day; I am enough, create my own reality, am happy and excited about life, am healthy and full of energy, am loved, and love myself.

I get up before the rest of my household and take space and time for just myself before the family blends their energy with mine.

So many ways to make self-care not just a routine but part of who you are. People will notice the radiating shine you carry with you because you put yourself first in a world where women are told that is selfish and should feel guilt over. No way! If you want me at my best, I have to nurture myself to get there first."
-Crystal

The Sisters Enchanted Community Member

SUGGESTED SELF-CARE ACTIVITIES
(for when you want to try something new)

● **Day 1:** Get outside and spend time in **NATURE**! It is so important to get fresh air, ground, and get moving! It's also great for stress and clears the mind.

● **Day 2:** Do something for yourself. Whether it's waking up before everyone else in your house and listening to the rain or sitting outside with your favorite cup of tea and a journal, do something just for yourself.

● **Day 3:** Try and take some time in the morning to pull an oracle card or tarot card. Whatever you like (or use an app if you don't own a card deck). Take a minute to think about it. Tuning in and focusing on yourself and your day helps pull you back to the center. Before bed, take some time to think back on what that card meant for you during your day. This is an excellent tool for self-reflection.

● **Day 4:** It's Time To Clean Out Your Closet! Get rid of the clothes that don't fit you or make you feel uncomfortable when wearing them. Only keep the items that empower you to feel confident and leave you smiling when you look in the mirror.

● **Day 5:** Do Nothing... just for a little bit, and forgive yourself if you fall off track a little on your 'do nothing' adventure.

● **Day 6:** Journal. Write down what you're grateful for, what you did yesterday, or what you want today to look like. You can journal on your daily card pull or use a prompt; it doesn't matter! Journaling is a great way to let some subconscious clutter out. Give it a try!

● **Day 7:** Drink more water! It is so important to stay hydrated. Start your day off with water before anything, and carry a water bottle around with you. Sip on some good old H_2O throughout the whole day. It aids in digestion, overall moisture in the body and skin, cellular turnover, and so much more. Water, not your thing? Add some fresh strawberries and basil or cucumber and fancy it up a bit.

CULTIVATE A QUEST PACK

PURPOSE OF A QUEST PACK

I've got a challenge for you.

If you carry a tote bag, purse, handbag, or something of the sort... dump it out. What's in there?

If you're like most people, you'll find:
- Crushed up granola bar
- Lip balm with some kind of somethin' stuck to it
- Pennies

If you're a person who loves all things crystals, cards, and nature, you may find some of that in there, too!

Looking through the items you carry with you every day, ask yourself, why is that in there?

I want you to carry a bag that you create with intention.
Life is crazy busy! Having a Quest Pack on hand will help you take your sacred space with you on to go when an unexpected moment arises.

It will serve as your reminder to make space for yourself, your vision, and your intuitive self to shine.

Instead of snacks that belong in a garbage pail, questionable beauty products, and loose change, I want you carrying around a **Quest Pack** that will support you in the *unexpected quiet moments, the inevitable chaos of life, and everywhere in between.*

GENERAL CHECKLIST

Some ideas for curating your Quest Pack:
- Your Quest Bag, tote, basket, backpack
- Journal and pen
- Water bottle
- Earbuds
- Snacks
- Oracle, Tarot, or Affirmation Cards
- Tokens of significance like crystals, jewelry, etc.
- Something cozy, like a blanket, shawl, sweatshirt
- Book, magazine, article to read
- Download a Podcast you want to catch up on
- Craft project, like knitting, that's easy to grab and go
- Pencil and paper to make a list, or write a letter to someone
- Coloring book and crayons or colored pencils
- Picnic blanket or beach towel

There is no wrong way to pack your Quest Pack! Do what feels right for you; pack things you love or things that you want to spend time learning or doing.

EXAMPLES

Looking to cast a future vision or design your path forward? Pack a **Quest Pack for Vision Casting.**

Here are some suggestions:
- Magazines or pre-selected images that align with the feeling you'd like your future to bring to your everyday
- Headphones and a set of meditations, visualizations, or

thought-provoking audio downloaded on your phone are
ready to be used
- A loose top that you can throw on to invoke the feeling of
  the future you are creating
- A journal and pen to write about the future
- Notecards or index cards and stickers or other easy to
  transport crafty goods to create affirmation cards to remind you of where you are going and that you are deserv-
  ing of going there

Looking to ground, center, and separate your energy from the world
around you? Pack a **Quest Pack for Reclaiming Your Energy**

Here are some suggestions:
- A shallow travel container with a lid filled with salt, a
  few drops of lavender oil, and dried lavender bits to use
  as a calming sensory experience on the go by drawing
  spirals in it and sending any unwanted energies away at
  the same time
- A journal and colored pencils or watercolor pencils to
  draw you and your energy map at the moment
- Some earthly elements like stones, shells, or acorns to
  hold and center yourself into the present moment and
  place on Earth
- Take your shoes off, and get your feet on some Earth
- Make a playlist of your favorite feel-good songs to listen
  to and envision your energy coming back to you with it
- Use a cord or string to weave your energy back together
  and align with itself
- Pick an affirmation to sit with, repeat, or write about
- Grab a crystal you want to work with. For instance, if you
  want to reclaim your creative energy, maybe you would
  take a carnelian with you to focus on

Wanting more creativity, joy, and playfulness in your life? Pack a *Creativity Quest Pack.*

Here are some suggestions:
- Child-sized scissors, glue stick, magazines, colored pencils, art pens...easy to carry art supplies!
- Music and earbuds
- A tunic/caftan/apron/or shirt that is flowy, colorful, and makes you want to twirl around with your arms spread wide
- Silly putty or playdoh to get your hands moving and your mind creating
- Cord or String to weave
- Needlepoint project
- Empty notebook for recipe creating
- Bring only 3 colored pencils or markers with you (*each a different color*). Challenge yourself to draw out your Quest spot using only 3 colors
- Bring Tarot cards, a pen, and some paper. Write a story. Pull one card at a time and use the card's theme to keep adding to your story, one card at a time.

Dreaming of more rest so you can receive whatever it is that your soul needs right now? Pack a *Rest and Receive Quest Pack.*

Here are some suggestions:
- An eye mask for napping during the day
- A cozy blanket
- A good book to get lost in
- A pen and paper for writing out your thoughts
- A deck of oracle, tarot, or affirmation cards to use as a journaling tool
- Journal prompts

- A bathtub quest pack!
- Bubbles
- Glass of wine or cup of tea
- Crystals
- A good book
- Playlist

HOW TO CREATE A SACRED SPACE TO ENJOY YOUR QUEST PACK

Creating Sacred Space can feel like this big thing that we have to get right. I mean, it is *SACRED*, after all.

A *Sacred Space* is a place that allows us to unfold. A place where we can be our truest selves, a place where we can focus on an intention or energy, or where we can just be still.

Here are some tips on setting the scene and opening the energetic gateway to your sacred space (*even if you're on the go*):

- Choose an item that you use to specifically open your sacred space — a tea that you drink, a candle that you light, a stone that you place in front of you, or a shawl that you wear. This is your indicator, your call to self and the universe, that you are in sacred space. You are listening; you are breathing; you are visioning.
- Visualize yourself closing a curtain around yourself. Anything within that visual is now your sacred space and yours alone.
- Carry a photo or printed image of a location that *FEELS* like sacred space to you. Pull it out, look at it, and close your eyes. See yourself there, in your sacred space.
- Put your arms out wide and turn in a slow circle a few

times. Draw your sacred space with your body. Pull your hands back into yourself. When you are ready to exit the moment, put your arms out wide again and spin the other way.

- When all else fails, put a "*do not disturb*" sign up and take a moment! You can make any moment a sacred one.

FINAL TIPS ON ACTUALLY USING YOUR QUEST PACK

For a Quest Pack to be useful to you, you actually have to use it! I don't want your bag sitting around collecting dust, so check out these tips on how to make sure you use your Quest Pack regularly.

- Show those around you the item you are using to declare your sacred space
- "*Train them*" to see that boundary when it is in place!
- Bring your Quest Pack everywhere. In the car for the grocery store, in your bedroom, or anywhere else. Sneak in those moments!
- Make it part of your weekly routine to clean out and re-fresh your Quest Pack, so you are always excited to use it again
- Make a group event of it! Have friends that might like something like this? Create Quest Packs that you can trade with one another and get fresh ideas and supplies without buying new things all the time.
- Try out different bags that work for you (backpacks, totes, crossbody, baskets, etc.)
- Put an alarm on your phone for moments when you are likely to pick up your phone and start scrolling to remind you to dig into your Quest Pack instead (lunch breaks, school pick-up, late nights, and early mornings)

"I treat myself to 'toes in the sand' days. Take an hour or so to find my way to the water's edge (lake, river, beach) and dig my toes in the sand. Just sit there and read a book, journal, meditate, stare into space. Whatever suits me at the moment. Picture the negative energy releasing into the Earth and water and healing, positive energy flowing in from my toes and filling me up. I kind of picture myself like The Star card in my Tarot deck."
- Naomie

The Sisters Enchanted
Community Member

Part Two:

CREATING THE PRACTICE

Days 8–14
Laying the Foundation for Self Care

Part Two: CREATING THE PRACTICE

Part One was an invitation to explore your current relationship with all the elements that detract from self-care. You set boundaries, identified barriers, and curated a relationship with time. The reflections from Part One will be the pillars that allow you to build nurturing practices into your every day.

In Part Two, you are being called to explore ideas, practices, and invitations as you embark on your self-care adventure.

You will dive deeper into what self-care is and begin looking at all areas of life as *opportunities for self-care*. In looking at four different types of self-care, you will see that even mundane life moments can be great acts of service to oneself.

At the beginning of this book, I asked you to consider the wild idea of looking at your whole life as a container for self-care. By the end of this section, you'll have the tools to do just that.

DAY 8: SELF-CARE AUDIT

To begin, let's first consider what you're already doing that is self-care, what you're thinking of as self-care, but it really isn't, and the difference between basic needs and self-care.

It's easy to confuse basic needs like bathing, eating well, and sleeping as self-care. These are fundamental pieces to any wellness puzzle. This is often the case for those who care for others, have responsibilities that affect others, or are stretched in all directions. Can these be a form of self-care? Sure, if that's the intention behind them.

Maybe you love taking a long shower and listening to an audiobook while enjoying the fancy body wash you hide from the rest of your family. That's not the same as taking a quick shower just to wash away the grime from yesterday. See the difference?

Similarly, shopping for new clothes to treat yourself before clearing out your closet or understanding what you don't like about what you currently own is probably more of an avoidance tactic than self-care.

The key to creating a life that is a container for self-care is looking for opportunities to turn the things you're already doing into self-care experiences.

What are you already doing that can be molded into a self-care experience? Maybe you already go for a walk every morning, but it's quick and not intentional. How can you add a *pause* to that?

Maybe you pay your bills every Tuesday. Is there a way to incorporate a ritual around this?

Maybe you light a candle in your house every day but never really think anything particular about it. How can you add another step to this? Turn it into an act of self-care?

Adding a **pause for intentional care** to what you are already doing is the easiest way to bring a self-care practice to life.

It's time for **a self-care audit**.

DAY 8 ACTIVITY: Do a self-care audit. What are you already doing that can be molded into intentional (and magical) self-care? What are you doing that you've been claiming is self-care but probably isn't serving that purpose very well? How do you know?

IDENTIFYING AVOIDANCE MASKED AS SELF-CARE

Ask yourself the question: How do I feel after doing this? Then ask yourself why do you feel that way.

Here are a few examples for you:

- If you go shopping as an act of self-care and then feel down on yourself afterward because you spent money you didn't intend to spend or realize you don't have room for the new items and now feel overwhelmed, this is probably avoidance. You are shopping to avoid feeling or experiencing something.
- Suppose you say no to an invitation and stay home instead to nap and read a book and feel guilty after. In that case, this is a matter of reminding yourself that you are worthy of self-care and not responsible for suffering to make others happy.

Asking yourself how you feel after doing something that you deem self-care will help you uncover any thoughts that need exploring.

DAY 9: PRACTICAL

PRACTICAL: *of, relating to, or manifested in practice or action; not theoretical or ideal* (Merriam-Webster Dictionary).

Practical self-care includes acts that don't fit the typical view of self-care but are a deep and essential form of caring for oneself.

Practical self-care looks like reading a book on money mindset, setting a weekly financial date with yourself, or saying no to things that stand in the way of your earning potential. Practical self-care can also be delegating one of your responsibilities to someone else or finally making the phone call you've been avoiding.

How is this considered self-care, and why are we starting with it?

So often, folks engage in self-care activities as a way of avoiding the tough stuff. Whether going shopping, taking oneself on a coffee date, or binge-watching your favorite show for a day, self-care used to avoid the hard stuff isn't doing you any favors. Sure, it's a great way to take a breath when you need one, but it's not a long-term self-care practice.

Engaging in a form of self-care that isn't about dressing up in bubble baths and cozy blankets is a way to remind yourself that you're worth caring for. You're brave, confident, resilient, and worthy of self-care because you're *you*.

Do the hard stuff first, and you'll enjoy the Instagram-worthy stuff even more later.

DAY 9 REFLECTION: Make a list of practical self-care ideas. Select a few to schedule over the next month!

PRACTICAL SELF-CARE IDEAS:

- Reading a personal development book
- Attending a webinar to learn more about money and wealth
- Getting your car checked over for safety
- Attending your yearly well-visit
- Decluttering your closet
- Setting up a payment plan for a bill you've been avoiding
- Creating an account that automatically puts money into savings

Incorporating Practical Self-Care time into your life will be the basis for creating a life truly built to support you. These efforts are the baby steps that lead to a better financial situation, improved health, and a less anxious state of being (*or whatever else it is that you are looking to create*).

DAY 10: SPIRITUAL

SPIRITUAL: *of, relating to, consisting of, or affecting the spirit* (Merriam-Webster Dictionary).

Spiritual self-care is crucial if you are working on connecting with your highest self, intuition, or past and future timelines (*exciting stuff!*). This can look like simply being and relaxing, journaling, and using tarot or oracle cards to come up with some great prompts for yourself, meditation, and more.

Spiritual self-care is an invitation to hear yourself talk, feel your body relay messages through sensation, and rejuvenate your energy.

This type of self-care is a beautiful experience, whether you're meditating or doing some inner reflection and being honest with yourself. It's just you, yourself, and you! Being your own greatest ally and own best friend comes through the release we find in spiritual self-care.

Packing your Quest Pack so that you are always prepared and ready for some spiritual self-care is helpful. There's nothing worse than stumbling upon a time when you're alone, thinking that you'd love to write in your journal or listen to that meditation you saved only to find that you can't find your tools. Have it all in one place and ready to go!

Other ideas include vision boarding, going on walks and sitting with the trees, taking a bath and listening to an energy clearing, or anything else you can think of. Anything can be a spiritual experience if you want it to be!

DAY 10 REFLECTION: Make a list of spiritual self-care ideas. Select a few to schedule over the next month!

HOW TO TURN THE MUNDANE INTO A SPIRITUAL ACT

It is said that 30% or one-third of most people's lives is spent working. Add to that necessary life tasks, cleaning, and sleeping, and a great deal of life is spent on mundane activities.

Looking for ways to create more connection, delight, and magic in these moments can do wonders for your spiritual practice and self.

Here are some ideas for turning the mundane into spiritual acts:

- Look for the energy of objects all around you and pause for connection
- Stop to ask, "what is my relationship to this..."
- Practice gratitude often
- Energetically clean while physically cleaning
- Release stagnant or negative energy along with the dirt

DAY 11: PHYSICAL

PHYSICAL: *having material existence; of or relating to material things; of or relating to the body* (Merriam-Webster Dictionary).

After practical self-care and spiritual self-care, it's time for physical self-care! This is an invitation to take care of your physical body.

Clean out your closet, so you have clothes that make you feel fabulous, deep condition your hair, get yourself a manicure and take care of your body!

Self-care for the body is a great way to relax, energize, and boost confidence. Intentionally caring for your physical body can also open you to feeling passionate about your body or encourage you to move it in a new and exciting way.

Taking a fun new exercise class, going for an invigorating uphill hike, or jumping in a pond for the first time in twenty years...all of this is physical self-care! Having fun with your body and remembering that you are perfect as you are is a real remembering of who you were and who you continue to be.

Your body and physical environment are sacred spaces; treat them that way.

DAY 11 REFLECTION: Make a list of physical self-care ideas. Select a few to schedule over the next month!

PHYSICAL SELF-CARE IDEAS:

- Treat your body as an altar and dress the way you want to feel
- Lay on the floor with your legs going straight up a wall to relieve stress
- Shake your body around, dance, or roll your head, shoulders, and hips to release stored energy

Quick note on physical body movement:

This isn't about physical fitness (*unless you want it to be, of course*). Movement helps to disperse energy, release stuck beliefs, and rewire your brain to be open to feeling flexible and optimistic.

Move your body in new and unusual ways to really start releasing everything that has been stored up.

DAY 12: RELATIONAL

RELATIONAL: *of or relating to kinship* (Merriam-Webster Dictionary).

Last but not least, we are talking about relational self-care. This is the kind of self-care that allows you to communicate your needs better and understand the needs of those around you. It can also look like connecting with others and developing supportive relationships that leave you feeling full and nurtured.

HOW DOES ONE DO RELATIONAL SELF-CARE?

Giving and receiving compliments with joy, understanding your inner self and how you react to a perceived conflict with others, investigating your astrology around communication and relationships, all of this is relational self-care!

Consider the boundaries discussion from earlier in this book. Setting, honoring, and enforcing boundaries comes down to *relationships and communication.*

Strengthening your ability to truly hear others will open the door for others to hear you.

Doing this type of work helps you understand your inner voice and where there is a disconnect between what you're thinking and what you're saying and between what you desire and the actions you're taking. It can also help you to set your boundaries and enforce them!

Here's the thing to remember, communication with yourself and with others will be so helpful in combating all the barriers that come your way when you're trying to prioritize self-care. You'll be able to talk yourself down when you see that you didn't set a boundary and are mad at others for standing in your way. You'll be able to forgive more easily as you navigate the path forward.

Practice self-care by working on your relationship with yourself and with others.

DAY 12 REFLECTION: Make a list of relational self-care ideas. Select a few to schedule over the next month!

CHALLENGE: Identify relational self-care activities that may be uncomfortable for you so you can prepare for them. Examples could include giving and receiving compliments or apologizing and forgiving. It could also be making decisions without asking for permission.

RELATIONAL SELF-CARE IDEAS:

- Ask questions instead of making statements
- Write your truth and practice speaking it
- Create a set of affirmation cards for yourself or to gift to others when you're struggling to find the words to say

Check out our free resources web page at 21dayselfcare.com to learn more about understanding relational self-care and communication through astrology.

DAY 13: WHEN?

When is it that you're going to do this coveted magical self-care?

There's no end to the research that shows the benefits of having a morning ritual, rising early, and setting the tone for the day. While that works for some, for others, that feels like an impossible task and maybe really is.

A helpful thing to do is consider time as a circle. When you draw a circle, you choose where it starts and ends. Think of your self-care time as the beginning of a circle. It's intentional and will create a break in the mundane, acting as a reset.

There is more information on this at the free resources web page: 21dayselfcare.com

Another piece to consider is your energy. When are you at your most creative or most likely to uphold a boundary? Suppose you are a caregiver, parent, or have co-workers, friends, or family demanding your time. When is it that you experience the least resistance to upholding your boundaries?

Suppose you have plenty of time on your hands and struggle with motivation. How can you anchor self-care around something else you are already doing?

Understanding your energy patterns, the rhythm of your day, and balancing that with when you can make time for your self-care is helpful.

SOME NON-TRADITIONAL IDEAS:

- Leaving for work a bit early or arriving home a bit late and spending time sitting by the water or going to a park
- Packing your lunch and bringing your quest pack on your lunch break
- Setting up your family for a weekly movie during which time you focus on yourself
- Finding someone to exchange child care or elder care with so you both have time for self-care
- Going to bed earlier and waking earlier

DAY 13 REFLECTION: Consider your barriers (the ones discussed on Day One) and when it is that you can make self-care happen for yourself. Get creative!

Use the circle on the next page to indicate the start of your 'self-care circle.' Shade it in and envision a 24-hour cycle with that marker as the start to your energetically refreshed day.

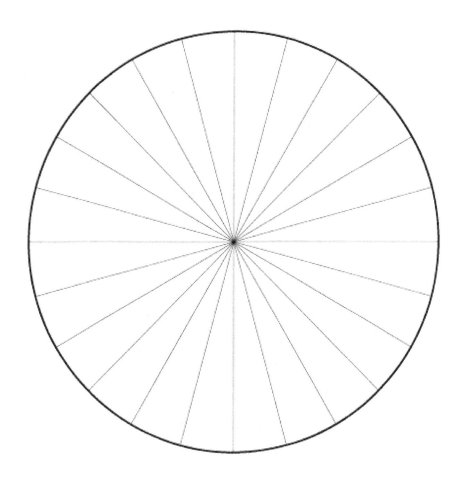

DAY 14: PLANNING

You've spent nearly two weeks diving into all things self-care and it's time to put this information to good use.

If you're new to trying to find time for yourself in the chaos of life then it can be helpful to go back to the boundaries page and consider why it is that you are serious about setting aside time for yourself to begin with.

What is your intention here? It's okay if it's just to do nothing for once! You have our permission (not that you need it!).

Maybe you have an intention to clear the voices of friends and family so that you can hear your own inner self for a change or maybe you really want to lean into your intuition and connect with your new favorite tarot cards.

Perhaps you're looking to dive into lunar energy and discover a rhythm to your day and life that wasn't previously there.

As you're putting self-care time on your calendar, consider your intention for this time. Knowing why you are setting it aside will help you to move through any resistance that arises and uphold your boundary. Having a *clear intention* will also help you to see yourself through anything that is masquerading as self-care that is really not (think shopping, eating lots of junk food, etc.).

DAY 14 REFLECTION: Open up your favorite calendar, schedule some reminders on your phone, set boundaries around your time and plan in your self-care for next week. Use this sheet to practice your *boundary setting* and *enforcement strategy.*

TIPS AS YOU PREPARE TO PUT SELF-CARE INTO ACTION:

Conversation Starters and Boundary Statements

- I need....in order to....
- At [insert specific time] I am going to...so that I am best able to...
- These are the things you can do while I...

Tips on identifying your intention

- Are you preparing yourself for a specific event or interaction?
- Is this time to keep you focused on your future vision be present, or release the past?
- What do you feel you need right now to gain clarity on life?

Be sure to go to the bonus resources webpage at 21dayselfcare.com for more information on identifying what you truly want versus what others have influenced you to want.

CONCLUDING DAYS 8–14

Growing up most of us aren't taught to create a life that feels spacious, supportive, and full of self-care.

Doing the deep work of understanding your relational, spiritual, practical, and physical belief systems and habits is a *lifelong journey*. On the bonus resources webpage that you have access to with this book, you'll find more helpful tools to aid you in this exploration.

One of the things many will struggle with here is getting others in your life 'on board' with your new way of being. You're not alone in this!

Remember that you can't change other people.

Focusing on yourself and creating a life that fills you up will inevitably cause a ripple effect that will influence those around you or else lead you down an *unexpected path* that may open the door to different relationships entirely.

You may also find that sometimes it feels too difficult emotionally to do some of the prompts that you encountered in Part Two. That's okay! Breeze through them and come back to them later when you have more capacity to complete them.

You've done lots of deep inner work here and it's time now to put it all into practice.

MORE SELF-CARE SUGGESTIONS TO TRY

● **Day 8:** Cuddle up with a book or a feel-good movie! It's okay to take some time and get lost in something that makes you feel good every once in a while.

● **Day 9:** Grab some sticky notes and write yourself love notes. Leave the notes in places you frequent so that you can remind yourself how amazingly awesome and beautiful you are.

● **Day 10:** Treat your body well. Eat more whole foods. Try your best to take care of your body inside and out. Your mind, body, and spirit will thank you! What things do you like to eat that leave you feeling awesome inside and out? Enjoy some today!

● **Day 11:** Spend the day with a loved one! Someone who lifts you up and fills you with joy and laughter. Raise your energy with like-minded friends. Whom do you like to spend your time with, who helps you to feel light?

● **Day 12:** What are you saying yes to today and what are you saying no to? Make a list! Do more of what makes your heart sing and less of what makes you feel overwhelmed and heavy.

● **Day 13:** When you take the time to make the things that you use to care for your body, your body will thank you! This is an opportunity to mix in some of your own MAGIC.

Make something for your body today even if it's as simple as putting some olive oil on dry skin or making an oatmeal and honey face mask. While you are mixing ingredients you can say an affirmation and add a sprinkle of enchantment to your daily routine.

● **Day 14:** Make a plan. Make a meal plan or schedule out your day. What's most important? What do you want to make time for? Making a plan for the day helps us to manage our work and play so we can be more productive and happy! How do you plan out your day? Are you even planning?

Part Three:

LIVING THE PRACTICE

Days 15–21
Laying the Foundation for Self-Care

Part Three: LIVING THE PRACTICE

The time has come to do your self-care!

Defining Success: What does it look like for you?

Before you move on, let's define what success looks like for you. As humans we are quick to avoid things we might fail at because we don't want other see us fail. Or, we don't celebrate ourselves because we think we aren't enough or aren't doing enough. Grab a pen and paper and write out *what success this week looks like and feels like for you.* Over the next seven days you'll be invited to put a self-care practice into place or do an act of self-care each day.

If you've gotten to this point in the book, that counts as a great success. Starting to think about self-care in a new way and thinking about how to create a life that is a container for self-care is a glorious step forward.

Getting distracted or forgetting about this book is not failure. It's just a thing that happens.

Looking for accountability? Go to the free resources webpage at 21dayselfcare.com for more information on finding community on your self-care journey.

DAYS 15–21 REFLECTION:

During Part Three you are going to practice self-care!

This is an invitation to consider your relationship with self-care, time, intention, and yourself. Over the next seven days try some new ways of being, different ideas for scheduling in your self-care time, and making it all happen.

Go back to everything you have read and discovered so far and use it.

Maybe you schedule five minutes of journaling time on one day and a two hour nap, book reading, and meditative walk session on another. Try a little bit of everything and see what works for you.

Take time each day to reflect back and see what barriers arose for you, what you ended up doing during your self-care time that didn't really feel like self-care, and consider all that came to pass.

In the end, developing a relationship with yourself and caring for yourself is the **ultimate act of remembering, rebellion, and witchery** and all of us at The Sisters Enchanted® want this for each and every person who wants it for themselves.

Onward!

DAY 15 REFLECTION:

Today is your first day of purposeful self-care! What do you plan to do for yourself? There are no rules here. Choose something fun or foundational, but make it happen.

Then, come back to reflect.

Recap your self-care plan including when it was to happen, what it was to be, and the intention for it:

Did you set a firm boundary around this time for yourself? Did you uphold it?

How did it go?

What worked and what didn't work?

What unexpected barriers arose?

What did you learn for next time?

DAY 16 REFLECTION:

It's the second day of self-care implementation, Magic Maker. Just reading this book has demonstrated a massive about of self-care but today I want you to schedule in something that will leave you giving yourself a pat on the back.

What's it going to be? Do it and then come back and reflect!

Recap your self-care plan including when it was to happen, what it was to be, and the intention for it:

Did you set a firm boundary around this time for yourself? Did you uphold it?

How did it go?

What worked and what didn't work?

What unexpected barriers arose?

What did you learn for next time?

DAY 17 REFLECTION:

You know that expression, third time's the charm? Well today is day three of our implementation week and whether or not days one and two left you feeling cared for or like you just can't seem to make time for yourself, remember that there's always a new opportunity on the horizon. And today is a new opportunity.

What act of self-care are you going to engage in today? Plan it in and then come back to reflect.

Recap your self-care plan including when it was to happen, what it was to be, and the intention for it:

Did you set a firm boundary around this time for yourself? Did you uphold it?

How did it go?

What worked and what didn't work?

What unexpected barriers arose?

What did you learn for next time?

DAY 18 REFLECTION:

You have entered the middle of your self-care implementation week! The first three days are behind you and the final three are still ahead of you.

For Day Four I invite you to indulge in something you wouldn't normally do. Celebrate all that has come to pass and get excited for the promise of the future.

Practice your self-care and then come back to reflect.

Recap your self-care plan including when it was to happen, what it was to be, and the intention for it:

Did you set a firm boundary around this time for yourself? Did you uphold it?

How did it go?

What worked and what didn't work?

What unexpected barriers arose?

What did you learn for next time?

DAY 19 REFLECTION:

Looking back on the first four days of this implementation week, what kinds of self-care have you practiced?

Choose something different or some aspect of self-care that you haven't enjoyed yet during this experience and schedule it in.

Afterward, come back to reflect.

Recap your self-care plan including when it was to happen, what it was to be, and the intention for it:

Did you set a firm boundary around this time for yourself? Did you uphold it?

How did it go?

What worked and what didn't work?

What unexpected barriers arose?

What did you learn for next time?

DAY 20 REFLECTION:

It's Day Six of your implementation week! Numerology tells us that sixes are a number of harmony and balance. Where could you use some harmony? In your living space, physical body, somewhere else?

Incorporate self-care around this (or something else if you'd like) and then come back to reflect.

Recap your self-care plan including when it was to happen, what it was to be, and the intention for it:

Did you set a firm boundary around this time for yourself? Did you uphold it?

How did it go?

What worked and what didn't work?

What unexpected barriers arose?

What did you learn for next time?

DAY 21 REFLECTION:
You've made it to the finish line!

However this journey has manifested for you, remember that small steps will lead to a life that feels like a container for self-care.

This is the final day of implementation week but it's **just the beginning for everything still to come.**

Practice self-care today and come back to reflect.

Recap your self-care plan including when it was to happen, what it was to be, and the intention for it:

Did you set a firm boundary around this time for yourself? Did you uphold it?

How did it go?

What worked and what didn't work?

What unexpected barriers arose?

What did you learn for next time?

THIS ISN'T THE END, IT'S JUST THE BEGINNING

Throw yourself a little party, Magic Maker, because you've reached the end!

My goal for you is to feel supported and cared for as much as possible. I want you to experience a life of self-care not just bits and pieces of it.

A job or career that fills your cup, relationships that are warm and cozy, and a mind and body that feel great to live in are my desires for you.

To really integrate all that you've learned and experienced into your being, I challenge you to incorporate a self-care gratitude practice into your evening routine. This might take as little as thirty seconds.

Fill in the blank to this statement each day:

"My self-care is a priority and I am grateful for _____."

Identify some act of self-care that you are grateful for each and every day and keep opening your pathway to implementing more of it, seeking more of it, and receiving more of it in your life.

If you've made it through this whole book without accessing the free resources webpage that accompanies this book, I encourage you to go to that page now. The material there will help you to expand on all that you've done during your journey with this book and more.

At 21dayselfcare.com you'll find:

- A video explaining exactly what an "Expedition to Soul" is
- Book Club Guide to use with others as you adventure through this book
- An alternative plan to use this material over a three month period rather than a three week one
- Examples of what it looks like to live a life that is a "container for self-care"
- Printable worksheets for the 'Reflection' portions of this book
- Examples of the activities where indicated in the book
- Optional 'Magic Tips' to incorporate a little enchantment into your practice
- Affirmations and a video guide on creating your own

And more!

You can find all of these resources here: 21dayselfcare.com

Thank you for taking this journey with us and may your self-care experience continue to expand each and every day.

Onward, Magic Maker.

ADDITIONAL SELF-CARE SUGGESTIONS

● **Day 15:** Turn on your favorite tunes and dance! Be the king or queen of kitchen dance parties. Cut loose, kick off your shoes, and dance. It helps push away negative energy, relieves stress, and is so much fun.

● **Day 16:** Be your own biggest fan. Be Yourself. Not everyone is going to like you and you aren't always going to feel like you fit in. But, being uniquely you is the biggest gift you can give to yourself and the world.

● **Day 17:** Treat yourself and eat something yummy! Don't ever feel guilty about having a treat. Life is hard. Don't shame yourself for what you eat, just say yes sometimes. And enjoy!

● **Day 18:** De-clutter. Minimizing what you have helps to de-clutter your home and mind. Go ahead and pick a room, closet, or basket and get to making some decisions on what's important to you, and what could be given away to better serve someone else!

● **Day 19:** Take a nap, meditate, or go for a walk. Whichever one of those things is something that you don't usually do to make space for yourself, do that.

● **Day 20:** Make a list of activities or practices that you are passionate about. Ask yourself if you have enough room in your life for the things that make you happy and leave you feeling expansive and alive. If not, how can you make more room for your passions?

● **Day 21:** Choose your own adventure! Conjure up three self-care ideas that you haven't yet tried. Then, schedule them in. The ultimate act of self-care is prioritizing yourself.

Here are a few more self-care tips that are a little less light but are so impactful when caring for yourself and your needs:

- Get a handle on your financial situation and set some money goals
- Go to bed earlier and eat slower
- Understand the expectations you have for yourself and for others and do an inventory on them to see if they are serving you or need to be let go (spoiler alert, most expectations aren't serving anyone)

- Get curious about what you fill your time and mind with - what TV shows you watch, what media you consume, how you unwind from a hard day - is this leaving you feeling cared for
- Investigate the words you use to describe yourself and begin to investigate the relationship you have with your inner and outer self

Magical self-care is both the light things we do for rejuvenation and the hard things we do so that we can move toward the future vision we have for our lives.

One final suggestion: write a letter of encouragement to yourself. Put it in an envelope with a stamp and your address. Give it to a friend or family member to mail to you at a random time of their choosing in the future.

ABOUT THE SISTERS ENCHANTED

In 2016 The Sisters Enchanted® began with a conversation and a dream. Founded by two sisters, Sara Walka and Anna Tower, this organization has grown to include a team of passionate teachers and supporters inspired to bring magic to the world.

At The Sisters Enchanted we know that living intentionally, leading with intuition, and making everyday magic will change your life and the world.

We believe in kindness and the innate power that each and every one of us is born with.

Wherever you are on your life's journey, make it an enchanted one here at The Sisters Enchanted.

AVAILABLE PROGRAMS

HOLISTIC WITCHERY
Holistic Witchery is the program that will change your life. This program walks participants through an exclusive framework for working with the lunar cycles, exploring your shadow self, incorporating magical practices into your life, and heightening your intuition through divination.

Coupled with community and unrivaled student support, Holistic Witchery is the program that everybody should gift themselves when they're ready.

EXPEDITION ASTROLOGY
A complete Certification program written and taught by experts in the field, Expedition Astrology is everything you need to know and more to deepen your connection with self, understand those around you, and even help others work through their own astrological blueprint.

This program is overflowing with live support opportunities from the teachers and will stretch you in all the right ways.

TAROT PROGRAMMING
In our Tarot Throwdown and Tarot Coach programs we guide learners to discover their own connection to the cards so that they can best hear the answers they already hold within them.

With thousands of tarot students worldwide, The Sisters Enchanted brings a unique form of tarot education to those who are ready to tell their story with the cards.

ABOUT SARA WALKA, FOUNDER AND CEO OF THE SISTERS ENCHANTED

Since 2016 Sara has helped thousands of women lean into their intuition, conjure joy, and make everyday magic. Sara believes that a little bit of enchantment, wonder, and mysticism goes a long way in creating a life that feels fun, purposeful, and spacious.

What began as a Tarot deck purchase at a Villain's shop in Disney World while on a school band trip has turned into over 20 years of witchery, self-discovery, and the wisdom that each and every one of us has the innate magic to create the life of our dreams.

As a homeschool mom, a self-made million dollar business owner, and recovering overachiever, Sara knows exactly how it feels to get lost in the day-to-day. That's why she makes this whole self-care thing simple, fun, and truly enchanting.

The Nitty Gritty: Sara is a psychic intuitive who always knew she was different from those around her. With a BA in English, a Masters in Education, and two minors in Psychology and Women's Studies, Sara brings her love of teaching, personal development, and witchery to all she does at The Sisters Enchanted. Prior to The Sisters Enchanted, Sara was a learning skills mentor for folks who learn differently and a consultant and advocate for school aged students with learning differences.

TRIP 4800?

JUNE
JULY
AUGUST
SEP
OCT
NOV
DEC

460   every 2

Sep 2 ~3000
Oct 4
Nov 4
Dec 2   one year

SARAH

70,000
- 5
65000
12,400

expenses on
ship
|||| D
4440
440 per day

Kevin #
— 12/22

24000
4800

43,600
3 500
39 100
28 800
10300
4000
4300
480

12/23   25600

2/24

Made in the USA
Coppell, TX
07 April 2022

76213175R00066